outdoor food

THE AUSTRALIAN
Women's Weekly

CONTENTS

AUSTRALIAN CUP AND
SPOON MEASUREMENTS
ARE METRIC. A
CONVERSION CHART
APPEARS ON PAGE 77.

Summer finds us all outdoors, enjoying the
long hot days and the warmth of the evenings.
The recipes in this book are just the type of
food we crave during summer – it's easy to
make, so there's no spending heaps of time
in the kitchen, and is simple to pack and
transport for a picnic or barbecue.

Pamela Clark

Food Director

POSH SAUSAGE SAMBOS

prep & cook time 45 minutes (+ cooling) serves 8
nutritional count per serving 21.5g total fat
(7.4g saturated fat); 1927kJ (461 cal);
38.2g carbohydrate; 27.1g protein; 3.5g fibre

8 thick lamb, rosemary and garlic sausages
    (680g)
1 loaf turkish bread (440g)
½ cup (140g) tomato relish
2 cups firmly packed watercress sprigs
caramelised onion
2 tablespoons olive oil
4 medium brown onions (600g), sliced thinly
1 tablespoon light brown sugar
¼ cup (60ml) red wine vinegar

1 Make caramelised onion.
2 Cook sausages in heated oiled large frying
pan until browned all over and cooked through.
Cool then halve sausages lengthways.
3 Split bread lengthways; spread top with
relish, spread base with caramelised onion then
top with sausage halves and watercress; press
bread top on firmly. Wrap sandwich in plastic
wrap or foil. At the picnic, cut sandwich into
eight slices.
caramelised onion Heat oil in large frying
pan; cook onion, stirring, over low heat, about
10 minutes or until soft. Add sugar and vinegar;
cook, stirring, about 10 minutes or until onion is
caramelised. Cool.
notes Sausages and caramelised onion can be cooked
a day ahead; keep, covered, in the refrigerator. Assemble
sandwich the morning of the picnic; wrap in plastic wrap
or foil. Cut into slices at the picnic.

PICNICS

PICNIC COTTAGE LOAF

prep & cook time 1 hour (+ refrigeration) serves 6
nutritional count per serving 24g total fat
(6.2g saturated fat); 2069kJ (495 cal);
43.1g carbohydrate; 23.8g protein; 5.4g fibre

1 large red capsicum (bell pepper) (350g)
1 large zucchini (150g), sliced thinly
   lengthways
1 medium eggplant (300g), sliced thinly
cooking-oil spray
1 tablespoon olive oil
1 large red onion (300g), sliced thinly
1 tablespoon light brown sugar
1 tablespoon red wine vinegar
1 round cob loaf (440g)
1 cup (240g) ricotta cheese
200g (6½ ounces) thinly sliced rare roast beef
20g (¾ ounce) baby rocket leaves (arugula)
rocket pesto
20g (¾ ounce) baby rocket leaves (arugula)
¼ cup (40g) roasted pine nuts
¼ cup (20g) grated parmesan cheese
1 clove garlic, quartered
1 tablespoon lemon juice
2 tablespoons olive oil

1 Make rocket pesto.
2 Preheat oven to 220°C/425°F.
3 Quarter capsicum; discard seeds and membranes. Roast, skin-side up, until skin blisters and blackens. Cover capsicum pieces with plastic or paper for 5 minutes, then peel away skin.
4 Place zucchini and eggplant on oiled oven tray; spray with oil. Roast about 15 minutes; cool.
5 Meanwhile, heat oil in medium frying pan; cook onion, stirring, until soft. Add sugar and vinegar; cook, stirring, until onion caramelises, cool.
6 Cut shallow lid from top of loaf; remove soft bread inside, leaving 2cm (¾ inch) thick shell.
7 Spread pesto inside bread shell and lid. Layer eggplant, cheese, onion mixture, zucchini, capsicum, beef and rocket inside bread shell, pressing layers down firmly. Replace lid; press down firmly.
8 Tie loaf tightly with kitchen string then wrap in plastic wrap; refrigerate about 2 hours or until required.

rocket pesto Blend or process rocket, nuts, cheese, garlic and juice until coarsely chopped. With motor operating, gradually add oil in a thin steady stream; process until mixture is thickened.

notes Instead of making the pesto, use a ready-made pesto of your choice; sun-dried-tomato or basil pesto would also taste great in this recipe.
You can use char-grilled vegetables from the supermarket or deli instead of cooking your own. Make sure you drain off all the oil before layering in the bread.

picnic cottage loaf

baked ricotta

BAKED RICOTTA

prep & cook time **40 minutes (+ refrigeration)** serves **8**
nutritional count per serving **17g total fat**
(6.5g saturated fat); 986kJ (236 cal);
10.7g carbohydrate; 10g protein; 0.9g fibre

500g (1 pound) fresh firm ricotta cheese
2 cloves garlic, chopped finely
½ teaspoon dried chilli flakes
½ teaspoon fresh thyme leaves
2 tablespoons finely grated parmesan cheese
2 tablespoons olive oil
125g (4 ounce) packet flatbread
90g (3 ounce) jar tomato tapenade

1 Press ricotta into 12cm (4½ inch) sieve;
place over bowl, cover. Refrigerate 4 hours
or overnight.
2 Preheat oven to 180°C/350°F. Grease oven
tray, line with baking paper.
3 Turn ricotta onto tray; sprinkle with garlic,
chilli, thyme and parmesan, drizzle with oil.
Bake about 30 minutes or until cheese is
browned lightly. Cool.
4 Serve ricotta with flatbread and tomato
tapenade.

notes The ricotta is best prepared and baked on the
morning of the picnic.
Any flatbread will do; pitta or mountain bread is fine.

turkish beetroot dip

TURKISH BEETROOT DIP

prep & cook time **50 minutes** makes **2 cups**
nutritional count per tablespoon **0.3g total fat**
(0.2g saturated fat); 67kJ (16 cal);
2g carbohydrate; 0.8g protein; 0.7g fibre

3 medium beetroot (beets) (500g), trimmed
1 teaspoon each caraway seeds and
    ground cumin
¼ teaspoon hot paprika
¾ cup (200g) yogurt
½ cup loosely packed fresh mint leaves
2 cloves garlic, crushed
1 tablespoon lemon juice

1 Boil, steam or microwave beetroot until
tender; drain. When cool enough to handle,
peel beetroot then chop coarsely.
2 Meanwhile, dry-fry spices in small frying pan
until fragrant; cool.
3 Blend or process beetroot, spices and
remaining ingredients until smooth.

notes This dip is delicious with toasted turkish bread.
Make the dip the day before the picnic; cover and
refrigerate until departure time.

honey and fig damper

CORN BREAD

prep & cook time **1 hour** serves **12** nutritional count per serving 7.3g total fat (3.9g saturated fat); 874kJ (209 cal); 27g carbohydrate; 7.4g protein; 3g fibre

3 trimmed corn cobs (750g)
¾ cup (180ml) buttermilk
2 eggs
45g (1½ ounces) butter, melted
1 cup (150g) self-raising flour
1 cup (170g) cornmeal
½ teaspoon salt
½ cup (60g) coarsely grated cheddar cheese
¼ cup finely chopped fresh flat-leaf parsley

1 Preheat oven to 200°C/400°F. Grease deep 22cm (9 inch) round cake pan; line base and side with baking paper.
2 Using sharp knife, remove kernels from corn. Process two-thirds of the kernels with 2 tablespoons of the buttermilk until smooth. Stir in remaining kernels and buttermilk, and eggs and butter.
3 Sift flour into medium bowl; stir in cornmeal, salt, cheese and parsley. Add corn mixture; stir until combined. Spread mixture into pan; bake about 50 minutes. Stand corn bread in pan 10 minutes before turning, top-side up, onto wire rack to cool.

note **Corn bread can be made the day before the picnic. Store in an airtight container in a cool, dry place.**

HONEY AND FIG DAMPER

prep & cook time **30 minutes (+ cooling)** serves **2** nutritional count per serving 13.7g total fat (8.2g saturated fat); 2817kJ (674 cal); 116.4g carbohydrate; 16.7g protein; 8.8g fibre

1½ cups (225g) self-raising flour
30g (1 ounce) cold butter, chopped coarsely
¾ cup (180ml) buttermilk
4 dried figs (60g), chopped finely
1 tablespoon honey
1 tablespoon self-raising flour, extra

1 Preheat oven to 220°C/425°F.
2 Sift flour into bowl; rub in butter. Add buttermilk, figs and honey to flour mixture; mix to a soft dough. Turn dough onto floured surface; knead lightly until smooth.
3 Shape dough into 8cm x 24cm (3 inch x 9½ inch) log; place on greased oven tray. Dust log with extra sifted flour; cut slashes into top of log. Bake 10 minutes.
4 Reduce oven temperature to 180°C/350°F; bake a further 10 minutes. Place damper onto wire rack, cover; cool.
Serve with **a selection of soft cheeses and dried figs.**
note **Damper is best made on the day of the picnic.**

corn bread

baby rocket quiche

BABY ROCKET QUICHE

prep & cook time 1½ hours (+ refrigeration) serves 8
nutritional count per serving 25.9g total fat
(15.6g saturated fat); 1375kJ (329 cal);
17.6g carbohydrate; 6.7g protein; 1g fibre

60g (2 ounces) baby rocket leaves (arugula),
    chopped finely
3 eggs
1 egg yolk
¾ cup (180ml) pouring cream
pastry
1¼ cups (185g) plain (all-purpose) flour
125g (4 ounces) cold butter, chopped coarsely
1 egg yolk
2 teaspoons iced water

1 Make pastry.
2 Preheat oven to 200°C/400°F.
3 Grease shallow 20cm (8 inch) round
loose-based tart tin. Roll pastry out on floured
surface until 5mm (¼ inch) thick. Ease pastry
into tin, press into base and side; prick base all
over with fork. Cover, refrigerate 20 minutes.
4 Line pastry with baking paper; fill with dried
beans or rice. Bake 12 minutes; carefully remove
paper and rice. Bake a further 8 minutes or
until pastry is browned lightly. Reduce oven
temperature to 160°C/325°F.
5 Place pastry case on oven tray; sprinkle
rocket into pastry case. Whisk eggs, egg yolk
and cream in medium jug; pour over rocket.
Bake quiche about 40 minutes or until set. Cool.
pastry Process flour and butter until crumbly.
Add egg yolk and the water; pulse until
ingredients come together. Knead pastry on
floured surface until smooth; cover, refrigerate
20 minutes.

notes Quiche can be made a day ahead; keep, covered,
in the refrigerator. You can also make and bake the
pastry case a day or two ahead, then add and bake the
filling on picnic day.

salmon and herb quiche

SALMON AND HERB QUICHE

prep & cook time 1¼ hours serves 6 nutritional count
per serving 11.4g total fat (4.8g saturated fat); 1049kJ
(251 cal); 14.1g carbohydrate; 22.3g protein; 1g fibre

3 eggs
2 egg whites
1½ cups (375ml) skim milk
½ cup (80g) wholemeal self-raising flour
1 medium brown onion (150g), chopped finely
20g (¾ ounce) butter, melted
2 tablespoons chopped fresh flat-leaf parsley
1 tablespoon finely chopped fresh chervil
¼ cup (20g) grated parmesan cheese
410g (13 ounces) canned pink salmon,
    drained, flaked

1 Preheat oven to 180°C/350°F. Grease deep
23cm (9 inch) round fluted pie dish.
2 Whisk eggs, egg whites, milk, flour, onion,
butter, herbs and cheese in large bowl until
combined. Add salmon; mix gently. Pour
mixture into dish; place on oven tray.
3 Bake about 50 minutes. Accompany with
lemon wedges.

note Quiche can be made a day ahead; keep, covered,
in the refrigerator.

POTATO SALAD

prep & cook time **45 minutes (+ refrigeration)** serves **8**
nutritional count per serving **30.4g total fat**
(4.1g saturated fat); 1764kJ (422 cal);
29g carbohydrate; 6.2g protein; 3.7g fibre

Cover 2kg (4 pounds) peeled potatoes with
cold water in large saucepan; bring to the boil.
Reduce heat; simmer, covered, until tender.
Drain; cut into 2.5cm (1 inch) pieces. Spread
potato on a tray; sprinkle with 2 tablespoons
cider vinegar, refrigerate until cold. To make
mayonnaise, blend or process 2 egg yolks,
2 teaspoons lemon juice and 1 teaspoon dijon
mustard until smooth. With motor operating,
gradually add 1 cup vegetable oil in a thin,
steady stream; process until mixture thickens.
Combine potato in large bowl with mayonnaise,
4 thinly sliced green onions (scallions) and
¼ cup finely chopped fresh flat-leaf parsley.

note **Potato salad can be made the day before the
picnic; keep, covered in the refrigerator.**

TABBOULEH

prep time **30 minutes (+ refrigeration)** serves **4**
nutritional count per serving **14.2g total fat**
(2g saturated fat); 790kJ (189 cal);
9.4g carbohydrate; 3.6g protein; 5.9g fibre

Place ¼ cup burghul in shallow medium bowl.
Halve 3 medium tomatoes; scoop pulp from
tomato over burghul. Chop tomato flesh finely;
spread over burghul. Cover; refrigerate 1 hour.
Combine burghul mixture in large bowl with
3 cups coarsely chopped fresh flat-leaf parsley,
½ cup coarsely chopped fresh mint, 3 finely
chopped green onions (scallions), 1 crushed
garlic clove and ¼ cup each lemon juice and
olive oil.

note **Tabbouleh is best made on the morning of
the picnic.**

SALADS

COLESLAW

prep time **10 minutes** serves **6**
nutritional count per serving **8.1g total fat
(1g saturated fat); 523kJ (125 cal);
8.8g carbohydrate; 2g protein; 4.5g fibre**

Finely shred ½ small cabbage; combine with
1 coarsely grated medium carrot, 4 thinly sliced
green onions (scallions), ½ cup mayonnaise
and 1 tablespoon lemon juice in large bowl.

note **Prepare coleslaw ingredients the day before the
picnic; keep, covered, in the refrigerator. Dress coleslaw
at the picnic.**

TOMATO CHUTNEY PASTA SALAD

prep & cook time **25 minutes** serves **10** nutritional count
per serving **15.6g total fat (9.7g saturated fat); 1555kJ
(372 cal); 42.3g carbohydrate; 14.3g protein; 2.2g fibre**

Cook 500g (1 pound) rigatoni pasta in large
saucepan of boiling water until tender; drain.
Rinse under cold water; drain. Meanwhile, cook
10 slices prosciutto in heated oiled large frying
pan until crisp. Drain on absorbent paper; chop
coarsely. Combine 1 cup crème fraîche and
½ cup tomato chutney in large bowl. Gently
mix in pasta, prosciutto, 315g (10 ounces)
halved cherry bocconcini cheese, 1 thinly sliced
small red onion and 1 cup coarsely chopped
fresh basil.

note **Pasta salad is best made on the morning of
the picnic.**

zucchini flower and tomato frittata

notes You need an ovenproof frying pan with a 17cm (7 inch) base for this recipe. If necessary, protect the handle of the pan by wrapping it in foil. You could also place the frittata under a preheated grill until set. Frittata is best made on the morning of the picnic.

ZUCCHINI FLOWER AND TOMATO FRITTATA

prep & cook time 35 minutes serves 4 nutritional count per serving 20.5g total fat (8.6g saturated fat); 1354kJ (324 cal); 6.6g carbohydrate; 27.6g protein; 2.3g fibre

6 baby zucchini with flowers attached (120g)
155g (5 ounces) reduced-fat ricotta cheese
8 eggs
¼ cup (60ml) milk
⅓ cup (50g) drained semi-dried tomatoes in oil, chopped coarsely
100g (3½ ounces) reduced-fat fetta cheese, crumbled

1 Preheat oven to 220°C/425°F.
2 Discard stamens from zucchini flowers; fill flowers with ricotta, twist petal tops to enclose filling.
3 Whisk eggs and milk in large jug. Pour egg mixture into heated oiled medium ovenproof frying pan. Top with zucchini flowers, tomatoes and fetta. Cook frittata over medium heat on stove top, about 5 minutes or until bottom sets. Transfer to oven; bake, uncovered, about 15 minutes or until frittata is set. Slide onto board; cut into wedges.

CHICKEN TERRINE

prep & cook time 1¼ hours (+ refrigeration) serves 8
nutritional count per serving 13.3g total fat (3.7g saturated fat); 1116kJ (267 cal); 0.8g carbohydrate; 35.7g protein; 0.5g fibre

14 slices prosciutto (210g)
625g (1¼ pounds) chicken thigh fillets
625g (1¼ pounds) chicken breast fillets
¼ cup (35g) unsalted pistachios, chopped coarsely
3 teaspoons dijon mustard
1 teaspoon finely grated lemon rind
¼ cup chopped fresh flat-leaf parsley

1 Preheat oven to 200°C/400°F. Oil 8cm x 20cm (3 inch x 8 inch) (5-cup/1.25-litre) loaf pan; line base and two long sides with baking paper, extending paper 5cm over sides.
2 Line base and sides of pan with prosciutto, slightly overlapping the slices and allowing overhang on long sides of pan.
3 Chop chicken into 2.5cm (1 inch) pieces. Process half the chicken until minced finely. Combine mince, remaining chopped chicken, nuts, mustard, rind and parsley in large bowl. Press chicken mixture into pan. Fold prosciutto slices over to cover chicken mixture. Fold baking paper over prosciutto; cover pan tightly with foil.
4 Place pan in medium baking dish. Pour in enough boiling water to come half way up side of pan. Bake terrine 1 hour. Carefully drain juices from pan. Cool, then weight with another dish filled with heavy cans; refrigerate overnight.
5 Turn terrine onto plate; slice thickly to serve.

notes Make the terrine up to two days ahead of the picnic. Slice the terrine before departure time or, better still, at the picnic.

chicken terrine

honey, soy and sesame chicken wings

HONEY, SOY AND SESAME CHICKEN WINGS

prep & cook time **45 minutes (+ refrigeration)** serves **4**
nutritional count per serving **10.3g total fat**
(3g saturated fat); 1233kJ (295 cal);
12.6g carbohydrate; 37.4g protein; 0.4g fibre

1kg (2 pounds) chicken wings
¼ cup (60ml) japanese soy sauce
2 tablespoons honey
1 clove garlic, crushed
2cm (¾ inch) piece fresh ginger (10g), grated
2 teaspoons sesame seeds
1 teaspoon sesame oil

1 Cut chicken wings into three pieces at joints; discard tips. Combine sauce, honey, garlic, ginger, seeds and oil in large bowl with chicken. Cover; refrigerate 3 hours or overnight.
2 Preheat oven to 220°C/425°F.
3 Place chicken, in single layer, on oiled wire rack over shallow large baking dish; brush remaining marinade over chicken. Roast about 30 minutes or until chicken is cooked through.
4 Serve chicken wings with a honey soy or sweet chilli dipping sauce.

note The chicken wings can be marinated a day before the picnic; keep refrigerated. Cook the chicken on the morning of the picnic.

DEEP-SOUTH FINGER-LICKIN' CHICKEN WINGS

prep & cook time **40 minutes (+ refrigeration)** serves **4**
nutritional count per serving **8.6g total fat**
(2.7g saturated fat); 1308kJ (313 cal);
21.2g carbohydrate; 36.9g protein; 0.8g fibre

1kg (2 pounds) chicken wings
2 tablespoons tomato sauce (ketchup)
2 tablespoons worcestershire sauce
2 tablespoons light brown sugar
1 tablespoon american mustard
dipping sauce
2 tablespoons tomato sauce (ketchup)
1 tablespoon worcestershire sauce
2 tablespoons light brown sugar
1 tablespoon american mustard

deep-south finger-lickin' chicken wings

1 Preheat oven to 220°C/425°F.
2 Cut wings into three pieces at joints; discard tips. Combine sauces, sugar and mustard in large bowl with chicken. Cover; refrigerate 3 hours or overnight.
3 Make dipping sauce.
4 Place chicken, in single layer, on oiled wire rack over shallow large baking dish; brush remaining marinade over chicken. Roast about 30 minutes or until chicken is cooked through. Serve chicken wings with dipping sauce.
dipping sauce Combine ingredients in small microwave-safe bowl; cook, covered, in microwave oven on HIGH (100%) for 1 minute.

note The chicken wings can be marinated a day before the picnic; keep refrigerated. Cook the chicken on the morning of the picnic.

tuna, sour cream and chive dip

LEMON AND GARLIC PORK RIBS

prep & cook time **40 minutes** serves **8** nutritional count per serving **20.2g total fat (6.1g saturated fat); 1404kJ (336 cal); 6.3g carbohydrate; 32.4g protein; 0.3g fibre**

1 tablespoon sweet paprika
2 teaspoons finely grated lemon rind
⅓ cup (80ml) lemon juice
2 teaspoons fresh thyme leaves
4 cloves garlic, crushed
2 tablespoons honey
¼ cup (60ml) vegetable oil
2kg (4 pounds) racks american-style
    pork spare ribs

1 Preheat oven to 240°C/475°F. Line two oven trays with baking paper.
2 Combine paprika, rind, juice, thyme, garlic, honey and oil in large bowl; add pork ribs, rub all over with paprika mixture.
3 Place racks on trays. Bake about 30 minutes or until well browned.
4 Cut pork racks into individual ribs to serve.

notes The racks can be marinated a day before the picnic; keep refrigerated. Cook and cut the racks on the morning of the picnic. Take lots of paper napkins and wet wipes for sticky fingers.

TUNA, SOUR CREAM AND CHIVE DIP

prep time **15 minutes** serves **8** nutritional count per serving **11.6g total fat (5.4g saturated fat); 995kJ (238 cal); 22.8g carbohydrate; 9.9g protein; 1.6g fibre**

125g (4 ounces) cream cheese, softened
185g (6 ounces) canned tuna chunks in
    olive oil, drained
1 tablespoon horseradish cream
1 tablespoon lemon juice
¼ cup (60g) sour cream
pinch caster (superfine) sugar
2 tablespoons finely chopped fresh chives
½ teaspoon finely grated lemon rind
250g (8 ounces) grissini (bread sticks)

1 Blend or process cream cheese, tuna, horseradish, juice, sour cream and sugar until smooth. Stir in chives and rind.
2 Sprinkle dip with some extra chives; serve with grissini.

note Make the dip the day before the picnic; cover and refrigerate until departure time.

lemon and garlic pork ribs

potted prawns with crostini

POTTED PRAWNS WITH CROSTINI

prep & cook time **25 minutes** (+ refrigeration) serves **4**
nutritional count per serving **57.3g total fat**
(34.9g saturated fat); 3202kJ (766 cal);
40.2g carbohydrate; 22.5g protein; 2.8g fibre

625g (1¼ pounds) uncooked tiger prawns (shrimp)
250g (8 ounces) unsalted butter, melted
½ teaspoon mustard powder
2 tablespoons finely chopped fresh chives
cooking-oil spray
1 large french breadstick (315g), sliced thinly

1 Preheat oven to 200°C/400°F.
2 Shell and devein prawns. Cook prawns in small saucepan of boiling water until changed in colour; drain. Rinse under cold water; drain.
3 Process prawns, butter and mustard until almost smooth; stir in chives.
4 Divide mixture between four ½-cup (125ml) ramekins; cover, refrigerate about 1 hour or until set.
5 Meanwhile, to make crostini, spray both sides of bread slices with oil, place on oven tray; toast in oven until browned lightly.
6 Serve potted prawns with crostini.

notes **Potted prawns can be made a day before the picnic; keep well-iced during transportation. Make crostini close to departure time.**

oysters with tomato and shallot vinaigrette

OYSTERS WITH TOMATO AND SHALLOT VINAIGRETTE

prep time **10 minutes** serves **4** nutritional count
per serving **10.6g total fat** (1.8g saturated fat); 543kJ
(130 cal); 1g carbohydrate; 7.6g protein; 0.3g fibre

1 tablespoon red wine vinegar
2 tablespoons olive oil
1 small shallot (25g), chopped finely
2 small tomatoes (180g), seeded, chopped finely
2 teaspoons finely chopped fresh flat-leaf parsley
16 oysters, on the half shell

1 Combine vinegar, oil, shallot, tomato and parsley in screw-top jar; shake well.
2 Top oysters with vinaigrette.

notes **Make sure the oysters you buy are freshly shucked, and keep them well-iced on the way to the picnic. Take the dressing to the picnic in a screw-top jar. Use either a red shallot or the french golden variety, and use a full-flavoured tomato – vine-ripened is good.**

PRAWN CANTINAS

prep & cook time 15 minutes makes 6 nutritional count
per roll 6.1g total fat (1g saturated fat); 844kJ (202 cal);
18g carbohydrate; 17.8g protein; 1.6g fibre

Shell and devein 18 uncooked medium king
prawns (shrimp). Combine prawns, 2 tablespoons
lemon juice, 1 tablespoon olive oil and 1 teaspoon
smoked paprika in medium bowl. Cook prawn
mixture in heated large frying pan, stirring, about
3 minutes or until prawns change colour. Whisk
⅓ cup buttermilk, 1 tablespoon mayonnaise
and 2 crushed garlic cloves in medium bowl
until smooth; stir in 125g (4 ounces) baby rocket
leaves (arugula). Cut slits in top of six small
bread rolls. Divide rocket mixture between rolls;
top with warm prawn mixture.

note **Prepare filling and make rolls on day of picnic;
wrap in plastic wrap and keep cool during transport.**

BEST-EVER CHICKEN SANDWICHES

prep & cook time 25 minutes (+ standing) serves 8
nutritional count per serving 15.5g total fat
(4.8g saturated fat); 1329kJ (318 cal);
23.9g carbohydrate; 20.1g protein; 1.5g fibre

Place 625g (1¼ pounds) chicken breast fillets
in medium saucepan; add enough cold water
to cover. Bring to the boil, reduce heat; simmer,
covered, 10 minutes. Remove from heat. Stand
30 minutes; drain. Cut chicken into 2cm (¾ inch)
pieces; combine in medium bowl with ½ cup
mayonnaise and ¼ cup coarsely chopped fresh
flat-leaf parsley. Spread eight slices white
sandwich bread with 45g (1½ ounces) softened
butter. Sandwich chicken mixture between
bread slices. Cut each sandwich into quarters.

note **The chicken mixture can be made a day before the
picnic, keep refrigerated. Make the sandwiches on the
morning of the picnic; wrap tightly in plastic wrap or foil.**

SANDWICHES & WRAPS

HAM, CHEESE AND TOMATO CHUTNEY WRAPS

prep time **15 minutes** makes **12** nutritional count
per wrap **9.2g total fat (5.2g saturated fat); 782kJ
(187 cal); 13.9g carbohydrate; 11.7g protein; 1.2g fibre**

Place two slices of white mountain bread
together; repeat to make four stacks of two
bread slices. Spread each stack with rounded
tablespoons of tomato chutney. Divide 60g
(2 ounces) baby spinach leaves, 2 cups
coarsely grated cheddar cheese and 315g
(10 ounces) shaved leg ham between stacks;
roll to enclose. Cut rolls into thirds crossways
to serve.

notes **Prepare the wraps the night before the picnic;
wrap each roll tightly in plastic wrap and refrigerate.
Cut the rolls at the picnic. You need 8 slices white
mountain bread for this recipe.**

LAMB WITH BABA GANOUSH AND ROCKET

prep & cook time **20 minutes** serves **8** nutritional count
per serving **7.7g total fat (2.5g saturated fat); 895kJ
(214 cal); 18.6g carbohydrate; 16.5g protein; 1.8g fibre**

Combine 500g (1 pound) lamb backstrap,
1 teaspoon finely grated lemon rind, 1 tablespoon
za'atar and 1 tablespoon olive oil in medium
bowl. Cook lamb in heated oiled large frying
pan over high heat until cooked to your liking.
Cover lamb; stand 10 minutes then slice thinly.
Spread inside of four pocket pitta breads with
250g (8 ounces) baba ghanoush; fill with lamb
and 60g (2 ounces) baby rocket leaves (arugula).

notes **Lamb can be prepared and refrigerated the day
before, but is best cooked on the morning of the picnic.
Fill the pittas as close to departure time as possible.
Baba ghanoush is a roasted eggplant (aubergine) dip
or spread. It is available from delicatessens and
most supermarkets.**

CARAMELISED ONION TARTS

prep & cook time **40 minutes (+ freezing)** makes **8**
nutritional count per tart quarter **10.9g total fat**
(3.1g saturated fat); 702kJ (169 cal);
13.2g carbohydrate; 4.2g protein; 1.3g fibre

20g (¾ ounce) butter
1 tablespoon olive oil
2 large red onions (600g), halved, sliced thinly
1 tablespoon light brown sugar
1 clove garlic, crushed
2 teaspoons fresh thyme leaves
1 tablespoon red wine vinegar
2 tablespoons water
1 sheet ready-rolled puff pastry, halved
6 cherry bocconcini cheese (65g), sliced thickly

1 Preheat oven to 220°C/425°F. Line oven tray
with baking paper.
2 Melt butter with oil in large frying pan, add
onion, sugar, garlic and half the thyme; cook
over low heat about 20 minutes, stirring
occasionally, until onion is very soft and
browned lightly. Add vinegar and the water;
cook, stirring, until liquid has evaporated.
3 Meanwhile, place pastry halves on oven tray;
prick all over with fork. Freeze 15 minutes.
4 Top pastry halves with caramelised onion,
leaving 1cm border; bake about 15 minutes
or until browned. Cool.
5 Top tarts with cheese; cut each tart into
four pieces; sprinkle with remaining thyme.

notes **Caramelised onion can be made a day before the
picnic; keep, covered, in the refrigerator. Finish making
the tarts on the morning of the picnic.**

smoked trout tarts

SMOKED TROUT TARTS

prep & cook time **40 minutes** makes **6** nutritional count
per tart **8.7g total fat (3.2g saturated fat); 748kJ (179 cal);
9g carbohydrate; 15.9g protein; 1g fibre**

cooking-oil spray
6 sheets fillo pastry
1 whole smoked trout (240g), skinned, flaked
½ cup (60g) frozen peas
3 eggs
¼ cup (60ml) skim milk
2 tablespoons light sour cream
1 tablespoon coarsely chopped fresh dill

1 Preheat oven to 200°C/400°F. Oil six 10cm
(4 inch) round loose-based flan tins.
2 Lightly spray one pastry sheet with oil; fold
into a square, then fold into quarters to form a
smaller square. Repeat with remaining pastry.
Line tins with pastry, press into sides; place on
oven trays.
3 Divide trout and peas into pastry cases.
4 Whisk eggs, milk, cream and dill in medium
jug; pour equal amounts into pastry cases.
5 Bake tarts about 20 minutes or until filling sets.

note **Tarts are best made on the morning of the picnic.**

caramelised onion tarts

choc-raspberry brownies

notes Make the brownie up to two days ahead and store in an airtight container. If using frozen raspberries, don't thaw them before adding to the mixture otherwise they'll bleed and won't retain their shape.

BERRY, ALMOND & COCONUT SLICE

prep & cook time 1½ hours serves 16 nutritional count per serving 11.6g total fat (6.2g saturated fat); 932kJ (223 cal); 25g carbohydrate; 3.8g protein; 1.9g fibre

2 cups (300g) frozen mixed berries
1 cup (220g) caster (superfine) sugar
1 tablespoon lime juice
90g (3 ounces) butter, softened
1 egg
⅔ cup (100g) plain (all-purpose) flour
¼ cup (35g) self-raising flour
1 tablespoon custard powder
almond coconut topping
2 eggs, beaten lightly
1½ cups (75g) flaked coconut
1 cup (80g) flaked almonds
¼ cup (55g) caster (superfine) sugar

1 Preheat oven to 180°C/350°F. Grease 20cm x 30cm (8 inch x 12 inch) lamington pan; line base and sides with baking paper, extending paper 5cm over long sides.
2 Combine half the berries, half the sugar and all the juice in small saucepan; stir over low heat until sugar dissolves. Bring to the boil, then simmer, uncovered, stirring occasionally, about 20 minutes or until mixture thickens; cool 10 minutes. Stir in remaining berries.
3 Beat butter, egg and remaining sugar in small bowl with electric mixer until light and fluffy; stir in sifted flours and custard powder. Spread dough into pan; spread with berry mixture.
4 Make almond coconut topping; sprinkle over berry mixture. Bake about 40 minutes; cool in pan, then cut into 16 slices.
almond coconut topping Combine ingredients in small bowl.

notes By spooning dollops of the almond coconut topping all over the slice, you will find it easier to spread evenly. Slice can be made the day before the picnic. Store in an airtight container in a cool, dry place.

CHOC-RASPBERRY BROWNIES

prep & cook time 1¼ hours serves 16 nutritional count per serving 15.4g total fat (11.5g saturated fat); 1304kJ (312 cal); 38.6g carbohydrate; 3.7g protein; 2.3g fibre

155g (5 ounces) butter, chopped coarsely
345g (11 ounces) dark (semi-sweet) eating
    chocolate, chopped coarsely
1 cup (220g) caster (superfine) sugar
2 eggs
1¼ cups (185g) plain (all-purpose) flour
½ cup (75g) self-raising flour
200g (6½ ounces) fresh or frozen raspberries
2 teaspoons cocoa powder

1 Preheat oven to 180°C/350°F. Grease and line deep 20cm (8 inch) square cake pan with baking paper, extending paper 5cm over sides.
2 Combine butter and 200g (6½ ounces) of the chocolate in medium saucepan; stir over low heat until smooth. Cool 10 minutes.
3 Stir sugar, eggs, sifted flours, raspberries and remaining chocolate into chocolate mixture; spread into pan. Bake about 45 minutes. Cool brownie in pan before cutting into 16 slices.
4 Dust brownies with sifted cocoa.

berry, almond & coconut slice

apple pie slice

APPLE PIE SLICE

prep & cook time **45 minutes (+ refrigeration)** serves **8**
nutritional count per serving **9.7g total fat**
(5.9g saturated fat); 1463kJ (350 cal);
58.6g carbohydrate; 4.8g protein; 3.4g fibre

1 cup (150g) self-raising flour
½ cup (75g) plain (all-purpose) flour
75g (2½ ounces) cold butter, chopped coarsely
¼ cup (55g) caster (superfine) sugar
1 egg, beaten lightly
¼ cup (60ml) milk, approximately
1 tablespoon milk, extra
1 tablespoon caster (superfine) sugar, extra
apple filling
6 medium apples (900g), peeled, cored, cut
　　into 1cm (½ inch) pieces
¼ cup (55g) caster (superfine) sugar
¼ cup (60ml) water
¾ cup (120g) sultanas
1 teaspoon mixed spice
2 teaspoons finely grated lemon rind

1 Make apple filling.
2 Grease 20cm x 30cm (8 inch x 12 inch)
lamington pan; line base and sides with baking
paper, extending paper 5cm over long sides.
3 Sift flours into medium bowl; rub in butter.
Stir in sugar, egg and enough milk to make a
firm dough. Knead on floured surface until
smooth. Cover; refrigerate 30 minutes.
4 Preheat oven to 200°C/400°F.
5 Divide dough in half. Roll one half large
enough to cover base of pan; press firmly into
pan. Spread apple filling over dough. Roll
remaining dough large enough to cover filling
and place over the top. Brush with extra milk;
sprinkle with extra sugar. Bake about 25 minutes;
cool slice in pan before cutting into squares.
apple filling Combine apple, sugar and the
water in large saucepan; cook, uncovered,
stirring occasionally, about 10 minutes or until
apple softens. Remove from heat; stir in
sultanas, spice and rind. Cool.

notes Apple filling can be made a day ahead; keep,
covered, in the refrigerator. Slice is best baked on the
morning of the picnic. Serve apple pie slice with
whipped cream. Ground nutmeg or cinnamon tastes
great stirred through the cream.
If you like, transport the slice, whole, in the pan and
cut into squares when serving at the picnic.

minted melon salad

CHOCOLATE HAZELNUT CAKE

prep & cook time 2 hours (+ cooling) serves 8
nutritional count per serving 37.5g total fat
(15.9g saturated fat); 2061kJ (493 cal);
32.1g carbohydrate; 8.2g protein; 2.3g fibre

155g (5 ounces) unsalted butter,
   chopped coarsely
155g (5 ounces) dark (semi-sweet) eating
   chocolate, chopped coarsely
5 eggs, separated
⅔ cup (150g) caster (superfine) sugar
1½ cups (150g) ground hazelnuts
⅓ cup (45g) roasted hazelnuts,
   chopped coarsely
chocolate ganache
⅓ cup (80ml) thickened (heavy) cream
100g (3½ ounces) dark (semi-sweet) eating
   chocolate, chopped coarsely

1 Preheat oven to 160°C/325°F. Grease deep
20cm (8 inch) round cake pan; line base and
side with baking paper.
2 Combine butter and chocolate in small
saucepan; stir over low heat until smooth.
Cool 10 minutes.
3 Beat egg yolks and sugar in medium bowl
with electric mixer until thick and pale; beat in
chocolate mixture.
4 Beat egg whites in small bowl with electric
mixer until soft peaks form.
5 Fold ground hazelnuts into chocolate mixture,
then fold in egg white, in two batches. Spoon
mixture into pan; bake about 1½ hours.
6 Cool cake in pan. Turn cake, top-side down,
onto serving plate.
7 Make chocolate ganache. Spread cake with
ganache; top with nuts.
chocolate ganache Bring cream to the boil
in small saucepan. Remove from heat, add
chocolate; stir until smooth. Stand 5 minutes
before using.

notes The cake can be made a week ahead; keep,
covered, in the refrigerator. Make and use the ganache a
day before the picnic. Keep the cake in the refrigerator
until departure time.

MINTED MELON SALAD

prep time 20 minutes serves 8 nutritional count
per serving 0.6g total fat (0g saturated fat); 326kJ
(78 cal); 15.7g carbohydrate; 1.3g protein; 2.2g fibre

½ small rockmelon (cantaloupe) (650g)
1 small honeydew melon (1.3kg)
1kg (2 pound) piece seedless watermelon
¼ cup loosely packed fresh mint leaves
½ cup (125ml) apple juice

1 Discard seeds from rockmelon and
honeydew. Using melon baller, scoop balls
from rockmelon and honeydew into large bowl.
2 Chop watermelon into small chunks; add to
bowl. Stir in mint and juice.

notes Use any combination of melons you like. Prepare
the melons a day before the picnic; keep, covered, in
the fridge. Add mint and juice to the melons at the
picnic. Keep cool during transportation.

chocolate hazelnut cake

BARBECUED CHILLI PRAWN AND NOODLE SALAD

prep & cook time 35 minutes **serves** 4
nutritional count per serving 5.9g total fat
(2.6g saturated fat); 1145kJ (274 cal);
21.4g carbohydrate; 30.6g protein; 5g fibre

100g (3½ ounces) bean thread noodles
1kg (2 pounds) uncooked medium king
    prawns (shrimp)
1 teaspoon finely grated lime rind
1 clove garlic, crushed
2cm (¾ inch) piece fresh ginger (10g), grated
2 tablespoons sweet chilli sauce
2 tablespoons lime juice
1 tablespoon fish sauce
1 small red capsicum (bell pepper) (150g),
    sliced thinly
1 medium carrot (120g), cut into matchsticks
1 small red onion (100g), sliced thinly
155g (5 ounces) snow peas, trimmed,
    sliced thinly
1 cup firmly packed fresh coriander leaves
    (cilantro)

1 Place noodles in medium heatproof bowl,
cover with boiling water; stand until tender
then drain.
2 Meanwhile, shell and devein prawns, leaving
tails intact. Combine prawns, rind, garlic, ginger
and half the sweet chilli sauce in medium bowl.
Cook prawns on heated oiled barbecue (or grill
or grill plate) until changed in colour.
3 Combine prawns, noodles, remaining sweet
chilli sauce, juice, fish sauce, vegetables and
coriander in large bowl.

tex-mex spareribs with grilled corn salsa

TEX-MEX SPARERIBS WITH GRILLED CORN SALSA

prep & cook time **40 minutes** serves **4** nutritional count
per serving **21.9g total fat (4.3g saturated fat); 2161kJ
(517 cal); 32.5g carbohydrate; 43.3g protein; 7.6g fibre**

**2 tablespoons light brown sugar
1 tablespoon dried oregano
2 tablespoons sweet paprika
2 teaspoons cracked black pepper
½ teaspoon cayenne pepper
1 tablespoon ground cumin
1 tablespoon garlic powder
¼ cup (60ml) water
2 tablespoons vegetable oil
1.5kg (3 pounds) racks american-style
   pork spareribs**
grilled corn salsa
**3 trimmed corn cobs (750g)
2 medium tomatoes (300g), seeded,
   chopped finely
1 medium red onion (170g), chopped finely
1 medium green capsicum (bell pepper)
   (200g), chopped finely
¼ cup coarsely chopped fresh coriander
   (cilantro)
2 tablespoons lime juice
1 tablespoon olive oil**

1 Combine sugar, oregano, spices, the water
and oil in large bowl; add pork, rub spice
mixture all over pork. Cook pork on heated
oiled barbecue flat plate until cooked through.
2 Meanwhile, make grilled corn salsa; serve
with pork.
grilled corn salsa Cook corn on heated oiled
barbecue (or grill or grill plate) until tender. When
cool enough to handle, cut kernels from cobs.
Place kernels in medium bowl with remaining
ingredients; toss salsa gently to combine.

chicken with bacon & pineapple salsa

1 Combine spices, oregano and oil in large bowl with chicken; toss to coat.
2 Make bacon & pineapple salsa.
3 Meanwhile, cook chicken on heated oiled barbecue (or grill or grill plate), until cooked as you like it.
4 Serve chicken with salsa and lemon wedges.
bacon & pineapple salsa Cook bacon on heated oiled barbecue flat plate until crisp; drain then chop coarsely. Place bacon in medium bowl with remaining ingredients; toss gently.

CAJUN CHICKEN WITH BACON & PINEAPPLE SALSA

prep & cook time **30 minutes** serves **4** nutritional count per serving 31.1g total fat (9.1g saturated fat); 2299kJ (550 cal); 10.5g carbohydrate; 56.4g protein; 2.9g fibre

1 tablespoon sweet paprika
1 teaspoon cayenne pepper
2 teaspoons garlic powder
2 teaspoons dried oregano
1 tablespoon olive oil
8 chicken thigh fillets (880g)
bacon & pineapple salsa
4 rindless bacon rashers (260g)
1 small pineapple (800g), chopped finely
1 fresh small red thai (serrano) chilli, chopped finely
¼ cup finely chopped fresh flat-leaf parsley
1 medium red capsicum (bell pepper) (200g), chopped coarsely
¼ cup (60ml) lime juice
1 teaspoon olive oil

GRILLED LAMB WITH SPICY PEACH SALSA & SPINACH SALAD

prep & cook time **25 minutes** serves **4** nutritional count per serving 24g total fat (8.1g saturated fat); 1793kJ (429 cal); 10g carbohydrate; 41.9g protein; 2.8g fibre

750g (1½ pounds) lamb backstraps
spicy peach salsa
1 small red onion (100g), chopped finely
2 large peaches (440g), chopped finely
2 tablespoons finely chopped fresh flat-leaf parsley
1 fresh long red chilli, chopped finely
1 tablespoon malt vinegar
spinach salad
75g (2½ ounces) baby spinach leaves
1 tablespoon malt vinegar
2 teaspoons olive oil
½ teaspoon white sugar
2 tablespoons roasted pine nuts
1 tablespoon dried currants

1 Cook lamb on heated oiled barbecue (or grill or grill plate) until cooked as desired. Stand, covered, 10 minutes then slice thinly.
2 Meanwhile, make spicy peach salsa; make spinach salad.
3 Serve lamb with salsa and spinach salad.
spicy peach salsa Combine ingredients in medium bowl; toss gently.
spinach salad Toss ingredients in medium bowl.

grilled lamb with spicy peach salsa and spinach salad

grilled citrus chicken with orange pistachio couscous

GRILLED CITRUS CHICKEN WITH ORANGE PISTACHIO COUSCOUS

prep & cook time **25 minutes** serves **4** nutritional count per serving **18g** total fat (4.4g saturated fat); 3620kJ (866 cal); 113g carbohydrate; 60.4g protein; 4.3g fibre

3 cloves garlic, crushed
1 tablespoon finely chopped fresh oregano
¼ cup (60ml) lemon juice
½ cup (170g) orange marmalade
2 fresh small red thai (serrano) chillies, chopped finely
4 chicken breast fillets (800g)
orange pistachio couscous
2 cups (500ml) chicken stock
2 cups (400g) couscous
2 medium oranges (480g)
2 green onions (scallions), sliced thinly
⅓ cup (45g) roasted unsalted pistachios, chopped coarsely

1 Combine garlic, oregano, juice, marmalade and chilli in medium bowl; add chicken, turn to coat in mixture. Drain chicken, reserve marmalade mixture. Cook chicken, covered, on heated oiled barbecue (or grill or grill plate), brushing with reserved marmalade mixture, about 15 minutes or until cooked.
2 Meanwhile, make orange pistachio couscous.
3 Serve couscous topped with chicken.
orange pistachio couscous Bring stock to the boil in medium saucepan; stir in couscous, cover. Stand about 5 minutes or until liquid is absorbed, fluffing with fork occasionally. Segment oranges over couscous; stir in oranges, onion and nuts.

note **Chicken can be marinated overnight, covered, in the refrigerator.**

chilli & honey barbecued steak

CHILLI & HONEY BARBECUED STEAK

prep & cook time **25 minutes** serves **4** nutritional count per serving **12.1g** total fat (5g saturated fat); 1354kJ (324 cal); 11.7g carbohydrate; 42.4g protein; 0.3g fibre

2 tablespoons barbecue sauce
1 tablespoon worcestershire sauce
1 tablespoon honey
1 fresh long red chilli, chopped finely
1 clove garlic, crushed
4 new-york cut beef steaks (800g)

1 Combine sauces, honey, chilli and garlic in large bowl; add beef, turn to coat in mixture.
2 Cook beef on heated oiled barbecue (or grill or grill plate) until cooked as desired.

note **Serve steaks with coleslaw or your choice of salad.**

BARBECUED PIZZA TRIO

prep & cook time **50 minutes (+ standing)**
makes **3 pizzas**

anchovy olive topping
nutritional count per slice **6.1g total fat**
(0.9g saturated fat); **598kJ (143 cal);**
17.8g carbohydrate; 4.1g protein; 1.3g fibre

pancetta topping
nutritional count per slice **10.7g total fat**
(3.4g saturated fat); **832kJ (199 cal);**
16.7g carbohydrate; 9.2g protein; 1.4g fibre

spicy sausage topping
nutritional count per slice **18.4g total fat**
(6.4g saturated fat); **1158kJ (277 cal);**
18g carbohydrate; 10.3g protein; 1.4g fibre

2 teaspoons (7g) dry yeast
½ teaspoon caster (superfine) sugar
¾ cup (180ml) warm water
2 cups (300g) plain (all-purpose) flour
1 teaspoon salt
4½ tablespoons olive oil
1 cup (250ml) tomato pasta sauce
anchovy olive topping
7 anchovy fillets, halved
¼ cup (30g) seeded black olives, halved
12 fresh basil leaves
pancetta topping
2 cloves garlic, sliced thinly
½ cup (40g) parmesan cheese flakes
6 thin slices chilli pancetta (90g)
spicy sausage topping
185g (6 ounces) cooked spicy italian
    sausage
1 fresh long red chilli, sliced thinly
¼ cup (30g) seeded black olives, halved
100g (3½ ounces) bocconcini cheese, sliced
2 tablespoons fresh oregano leaves

1 To make pizza dough, combine yeast, sugar
and the water in small bowl; cover, stand in
warm place about 10 minutes or until frothy.
Sift flour and salt into large bowl; stir in yeast
mixture and 2 tablespoons of the oil; mix to a
soft dough. Bring dough together with your
hands and add a little extra water, if needed,
until ingredients are combined.
2 Knead dough on floured surface about
10 minutes or until smooth and elastic. Place
dough in lightly oiled large bowl; cover, stand in
warm place about 1 hour or until doubled in size.
3 Meanwhile, preheat a covered barbecue.
4 Punch dough down with your fist, then knead
on lightly floured surface until smooth. Divide
dough into three portions. Roll each portion into
16cm x 40cm (6½ inch x 16 inch) rectangle.
5 Layer two pieces of foil large enough to fit one
rectangle of dough. Brush foil with 1 teaspoon
of the remaining oil; place one portion of dough
on top of foil. Repeat process with extra foil, oil
and dough to make a further two pizza bases.
6 Turn off burners underneath middle grill
plate, leaving outer burners on to cook by
indirect heat. Place pizzas on foil on grill plate;
cover barbecue, cook about 4 minutes or until
underneath is browned. (If dough puffs up,
flatten quickly with an egg slide.)
7 Carefully remove bases from barbecue,
close cover. Turn pizza bases over on foil,
brush cooked sides with remaining oil, then
spread each base with one-third of the tomato
pasta sauce. Top with selected ingredients for
each topping except the fresh herbs. Return
pizzas to barbecue on foil; cover barbecue,
cook 5 minutes or until browned underneath
and crisp. Serve pizzas sprinkled with herbs.

notes This dough recipe makes enough for three thin
pizza bases. Each topping recipe makes enough to
cover one base. Cut each pizza into five slices to serve.

lamb chops with capsicum mayo & fetta olive mash

LAMB CHOPS WITH CAPSICUM MAYO & FETTA OLIVE MASH

prep & cook time **25 minutes** serves **4** nutritional count per serving **46.7g total fat (19.4g saturated fat); 3348kJ (801 cal); 40.2g carbohydrate; 47.1g protein; 4g fibre**

1kg (2 pounds) potatoes, chopped coarsely
⅔ cup (160ml) warmed buttermilk
200g (6½ ounces) fetta cheese, crumbled
½ cup (60g) thinly sliced seeded black olives
1 tablespoon olive oil
100g (3½ ounces) roasted red capsicum
  (bell pepper)
½ cup (150g) mayonnaise
8 lamb mid-loin chops (800g)

1 Boil, steam or microwave potato until tender; drain. Mash potato with buttermilk until smooth. Stir in cheese, olives then drizzle with olive oil.
2 Blend or process capsicum and mayonnaise until smooth.
3 Cook lamb on heated oiled barbecue (or grill or grill plate) until cooked as desired.
4 Top lamb with capsicum mayonnaise; serve with fetta olive mash.

PORK CUTLETS WITH FENNEL APPLE RELISH

prep & cook time **35 minutes** serves **4** nutritional count per serving **39.2g total fat (17.2g saturated fat); 2909kJ (696 cal); 44.2 g carbohydrate; 38.1g protein; 7.7g fibre**

2 tablespoons cider vinegar
1 tablespoon dijon mustard
¼ cup (60ml) olive oil
2 teaspoons caster (superfine) sugar
4 pork cutlets (940g)
1kg (2 pounds) unpeeled baby new potatoes
½ cup (120g) sour cream
45g (1½ ounces) butter, softened
¼ cup chopped fresh flat-leaf parsley
2 tablespoons coarsely chopped fresh dill
fennel apple relish
1 large unpeeled green apple (200g),
  chopped finely
1 small red onion (100g), chopped finely
1 medium fennel bulb (300g), trimmed,
  chopped finely

1 To make dressing, whisk vinegar, mustard, oil and sugar in medium bowl. Combine pork and 2 tablespoons of the dressing in large bowl. Reserve remaining dressing.
2 Make fennel apple relish.
3 Drain pork; reserve marinade. Cook pork on heated oiled barbecue (or grill or grill plate) until browned both sides and cooked as desired, brushing with marinade occasionally.
4 Meanwhile, boil, steam or microwave potatoes until tender; drain. Mash half the potatoes with sour cream and butter in large bowl until smooth; stir in herbs. Using back of fork, roughly crush remaining potatoes until skins burst and flesh is just crushed; stir into herbed mash.
5 Serve pork with relish and herbed potato.
fennel apple relish Combine apple, onion and fennel in bowl with remaining dressing.

note **Pork can be marinated overnight, covered, in the refrigerator.**

pork cutlets with fennel apple relish

barbecued fish with vegetable parcels

BARBECUED FISH WITH VEGETABLE PARCELS

prep & cook time **1 hour** serves **8** nutritional count
per serving 24.2g total fat (14.5g saturated fat); 1664kJ
(398 cal); 12.4g carbohydrate; 30.9g protein; 4.2g fibre

1 whole fish (2kg)
1 clove garlic, sliced thinly
3 sprigs fresh rosemary, cut into 2.5cm
(1 inch) lengths
1 medium lemon (140g), sliced thinly
45g (1½ ounces) butter
2 large zucchini (300g)
2 trimmed corn cobs (500g), sliced thickly
2 medium red capsicums (bell peppers)
(400g), sliced thickly
1 large red onion (300g), cut into wedges
lemon herb butter
155g (5 ounces) butter, softened
1 clove garlic, crushed
2 teaspoons finely grated lemon rind
2 teaspoons finely chopped fresh rosemary

1 Make lemon herb butter.
2 Score fish both sides through thickest part of flesh. Push garlic and rosemary into cuts; fill cavity with a third of the lemon slices.
3 Place a long piece of baking paper on bench; place half the remaining lemon slices on paper. Place fish on lemon; top with remaining lemon then butter. Fold paper over fish to completely enclose, then wrap tightly in foil.
4 Cook fish on heated oiled barbecue (or grill or grill plate) 20 minutes; turn, cook about 20 minutes.
5 Meanwhile, cut zucchini in half crossways; cut each half lengthways into six pieces. Combine zucchini with remaining ingredients in large bowl. Place eight 30cm (12 inch) foil squares on bench; divide vegetable mixture among foil squares. Gather corners of squares together; fold to enclose vegetables securely.
6 Cook parcels on heated barbecue flat plate until vegetables are tender.
7 Open vegetable parcels; top with slices of lemon herb butter. Serve with fish.
lemon herb butter Combine ingredients in small bowl. Place on piece of plastic wrap; shape into 6cm (2¼ inch) log, wrap tightly. Freeze until firm; cut into eight slices.

note We used snapper in this recipe, but a fish like salmon would work well, too – though it may need slightly less cooking time.

steak sandwich

STEAK SANDWICH

prep & cook time **30 minutes** makes **4** nutritional count per sandwich 20.5g total fat (5g saturated fat); 2809kJ (672 cal); 78.1g carbohydrate; 39.7g protein; 6.4g fibre

2 cloves garlic, crushed
2 tablespoons olive oil
4 thin beef scotch fillet steaks (500g)
2 medium brown onions (200g), sliced thinly
1 tablespoon light brown sugar
1 tablespoon balsamic vinegar
8 thick slices sourdough bread (560g)
1 baby cos lettuce (180g), leaves separated
2 dill pickles (40g) sliced thinly
¼ cup (80g) tomato chutney

1 Combine garlic and half the oil in medium bowl; add beef, rub both sides with mixture.
2 Heat remaining oil on barbecue flat plate; cook onion over low heat, stirring occasionally, about 10 minutes or until soft. Add sugar and vinegar; cook, stirring, about 5 minutes or until onion is caramelised.
3 Meanwhile, cook beef on heated oiled barbecue (or grill or grill plate).
4 Toast bread both sides on barbecue. Sandwich lettuce, steaks, onion, pickle and chutney between toast slices.

GRILLED BEEF BURGERS WITH EGGPLANT AND HUMMUS

prep & cook time **25 minutes** serves **4** nutritional count per serving 21.2g total fat (6.2g saturated fat); 2913kJ (697 cal); 71.6g carbohydrate; 48.1g protein; 12.6g fibre

625g (1¼ pounds) beef mince
2 teaspoons ground cumin
2 cloves garlic, crushed
¼ cup finely chopped fresh coriander (cilantro)
4 baby eggplants (240g), sliced thickly
3 medium egg (plum) tomatoes (225g),
    sliced thickly
1 medium brown onion (150g), sliced thinly
½ cup (130g) hummus
2 teaspoons lemon juice
1 teaspoon olive oil
8 thick slices sourdough bread (560g)
100g (3½ ounces) rocket (arugula), trimmed

grilled beef burgers with eggplant and hummus

1 Combine beef, cumin, garlic and coriander in medium bowl; shape mixture into four patties.
2 Cook patties, eggplant, tomato and onion, in batches, on heated oiled barbecue (or grill or grill plate) until patties are cooked through and eggplant is tender.
3 Meanwhile, combine hummus, juice and oil in small bowl.
4 Toast bread both sides on barbecue.
5 Sandwich rocket, eggplant, patties, tomato, hummus and onion between toast slices.

char-grilled salmon with avocado salsa

VEAL CUTLETS WITH GREEN OLIVE SALSA

prep & cook time **35 minutes** serves **4** nutritional count per serving **16.3g total fat (2.7g saturated fat); 1112kJ (266 cal); 5.8g carbohydrate; 23.4g protein; 1.2g fibre**

2 tablespoons olive oil
2 cloves garlic, crushed
1 tablespoon finely chopped fresh oregano
2 teaspoons finely grated lemon rind
1 tablespoon lemon juice
4 veal cutlets (500g)
green olive salsa
1 tablespoon lemon juice
¼ cup chopped fresh flat-leaf parsley
½ cup (80g) finely chopped large green olives
1 small green capsicum (bell pepper) (150g), chopped finely
1 tablespoon olive oil
1 clove garlic, crushed
1 tablespoon finely chopped fresh oregano

1 Combine oil, garlic, oregano, rind and juice in small bowl; brush mixture over veal. Cook veal on heated oiled barbecue (or grill or grill plate) until cooked as desired.
2 Meanwhile, make green olive salsa; serve veal with salsa.
green olive salsa Combine ingredients in small bowl.

Serve with **barbecued kipfler potatoes.**

CHAR-GRILLED SALMON WITH AVOCADO SALSA

prep & cook time **25 minutes** serves **4** nutritional count per serving **46.7g total fat (6.9g saturated fat); 2261kJ (541 cal); 3g carbohydrate; 41g protein; 1.6g fibre**

4 salmon fillets (800g)
¼ cup (60ml) lemon juice
¼ cup (60ml) olive oil
75g (2½ ounces) baby rocket leaves (arugula)
avocado salsa
1 large avocado (320g), sliced thickly
1 small red onion (100g), sliced thinly
2 tablespoons coarsely chopped fresh dill
2 tablespoons rinsed, drained baby capers

1 Cook salmon on heated oiled barbecue (or grill or grill plate).
2 Meanwhile, make avocado salsa.
3 To make dressing, combine juice and oil in screw-top jar; shake well.
4 Serve salmon on rocket with avocado salsa; drizzle with dressing.
avocado salsa Combine ingredients in medium bowl.

veal cutlets with green olive salsa

felafel burgers

FELAFEL BURGERS

prep & cook time **25 minutes** serves **4** nutritional count
per serving **13.9g total fat (2.4g saturated fat); 2195kJ
(525 cal); 71.2g carbohydrate; 22.6g protein; 10.9g fibre**

625g (1¼ pounds) canned chickpeas
   (garbanzo), rinsed, drained
1 medium brown onion (150g),
   chopped coarsely
2 cloves garlic, quartered
½ cup chopped fresh flat-leaf parsley
2 teaspoons ground coriander
1 teaspoon ground cumin
1 teaspoon bicarbonate of soda (baking soda)
2 tablespoons plain (all-purpose) flour
1 egg
1 loaf turkish bread (440g)
1 large tomato (220g), sliced thinly
20g (¾ ounce) rocket leaves (arugula)
yogurt and tahini sauce
¼ cup (70g) yogurt
2 tablespoons tahini
1 tablespoon lemon juice

1 Blend or process chickpeas, onion, garlic,
parsley, coriander, cumin, soda, flour and egg
until almost smooth. Shape mixture into four
patties. Cook patties on heated oiled barbecue
flat plate (or grill or grill plate) about 10 minutes
or until browned both sides.
2 Cut bread into quarters; toast both sides on
heated oiled grill plate (or grill or barbecue).
3 Meanwhile, make yogurt and tahini sauce.
4 Split each piece of bread in half horizontally;
sandwich sauce, tomato, patties and rocket
between bread halves.
yogurt and tahini sauce Combine ingredients
in small bowl.

note **When cooking felafel, use two spatulas to turn
them carefully, so they don't break.**

butterflied lamb with fresh mint sauce

BUTTERFLIED LAMB WITH FRESH MINT SAUCE

prep & cook time **40 minutes**
(+ refrigeration and standing) serves **10**
nutritional count per serving **8.1g total fat**
(3.6g saturated fat); 1166kJ (279 cal);
18.2g carbohydrate; 32.9g protein; 0.2g fibre

½ cup (90g) honey
1 tablespoon wholegrain mustard
2kg (4 pound) butterflied leg of lamb
¼ cup loosely packed fresh rosemary sprigs
mint sauce
½ cup (125ml) water
½ cup (110g) firmly packed light brown sugar
1½ cups (375ml) cider vinegar
½ cup finely chopped fresh mint

1 Make mint sauce.
2 Combine a quarter of the mint sauce, honey and mustard in large shallow dish; add lamb, turn to coat in marinade. Cover; refrigerate 3 hours or overnight, turning occasionally. Refrigerate remaining mint sauce separately.
3 Drain lamb; place, fat-side down, on heated oiled barbecue (or grill or grill plate). Cover lamb loosely with foil; cook about 10 minutes or until browned underneath. Uncover; turn lamb, sprinkle with rosemary. Cook, covered, about 10 minutes or until cooked as desired (or cook by indirect heat in covered barbecue following manufacturer's instructions). Remove from heat; stand, covered, 15 minutes.
4 Slice lamb thinly; serve with remaining mint sauce.

mint sauce Combine the water and sugar in small saucepan. Stir over heat, without boiling, until sugar dissolves. Bring to the boil, then simmer, uncovered, without stirring, about 5 minutes or until syrup thickens slightly. Combine syrup, vinegar and mint in small bowl.
Serve with **a tomato and radish salad.**

notes **The mint sauce can be made several days ahead. Ask your butcher to butterfly a leg of lamb for you – it's far easier than doing it at home.**

beef teriyaki platter

BEEF TERIYAKI PLATTER

prep & cook time **30 minutes (+ refrigeration)** serves **4**
nutritional count per serving **9.3g total fat**
(3.8g saturated fat); 1032kJ (247 cal);
3.5g carbohydrate; 36.1g protein; 2g fibre

⅓ cup (80ml) teriyaki sauce
2.5cm (1 inch) piece fresh ginger (15g), grated
1 clove garlic, crushed
3 new york cut beef steaks (600g), trimmed
500g (1 pound) asparagus, trimmed
8 green onions (scallions), trimmed
1 teaspoon wasabi paste
¼ cup (60ml) japanese soy sauce

1 Combine teriyaki sauce, ginger, garlic and beef in large bowl. Cover; refrigerate 3 hours or overnight.
2 Cook beef on heated oiled barbecue (or grill or grill plate). Remove from heat, cover; stand 5 minutes before cutting thinly.
3 Cook asparagus and onion on heated oiled barbecue until tender.
4 Serve beef with vegetables; accompany with combined wasabi and soy sauce.

SPICED LAMB CUTLETS WITH TOMATO AND PARSLEY SALAD

prep & cook time **25 minutes** serves **4** nutritional count per serving **9.6g total fat (3.2g saturated fat); 807kJ (193 cal); 2.5g carbohydrate; 22.7g protein; 2g fibre**

Combine 2 teaspoons each ground cumin and ground coriander with 12 french-trimmed lamb cutlets in medium bowl. Cook lamb and 4 quartered medium egg (plum) tomatoes on heated oiled barbecue (or grill or grill plate). To make salad, combine tomato with 1 coarsely chopped lebanese cucumber, ½ cup reduced-fat cottage cheese, 1 cup loosely packed fresh flat-leaf parsley leaves, 2 teaspoons olive oil, 2 tablespoons red wine vinegar and 1 crushed garlic clove in medium bowl. Serve lamb with tomato and parsley salad.

MONGOLIAN LAMB CUTLETS

prep & cook time **15 minutes (+ refrigeration)** serves **4** nutritional count per serving **14.9g total fat (5.4g saturated fat); 949kJ (227 cal); 5.4g carbohydrate; 13.4g protein; 0.2g fibre**

Combine 1 tablespoon white sugar, ⅓ cup japanese soy sauce, ⅓ cup dry sherry and 1 tablespoon sesame oil in large bowl; add 12 french-trimmed lamb cutlets, turn to coat in marinade. Cover; refrigerate 3 hours or overnight. Cut green stem from 3 green onions (scallions) into four even lengths; slice each piece lengthways into thin strips. Place strips in small bowl of iced water; refrigerate about 20 minutes or until curled. Drain lamb over medium saucepan; bring marinade to the boil. Reduce heat; simmer, uncovered, until marinade is reduced by half. Meanwhile, cook lamb on heated oiled barbecue (or grill or grill plate) until cooked as desired. Serve lamb brushed with marinade and sprinkled with onion curls.

LAMB CUTLETS

DUKKAH-CRUSTED CUTLETS WITH ROASTED GARLIC YOGURT

prep & cook time **30 minutes** serves **4** nutritional count per serving **27.8g total fat (8.7g saturated fat); 1547kJ (370 cal); 5.7g carbohydrate; 22.9g protein; 2.9g fibre**

Preheat oven to 180°C/350°F. Place 6 unpeeled garlic cloves on oven tray; drizzle with 1 teaspoon vegetable oil. Roast 10 minutes. Peel garlic then crush in small bowl with 1 cup yogurt. Cover; refrigerate. To make dukkah, blend or process 2 tablespoons each roasted hazelnuts and roasted unsalted pistachios until chopped finely. Dry-fry 2 tablespoons ground coriander, 2 tablespoons sesame seeds and 1 tablespoon ground cumin in small frying pan until fragrant; combine with nuts in medium bowl. Add 12 french-trimmed lamb cutlets; turn to coat in dukkah mixture. Cook lamb on heated oiled barbecue (or grill or grill plate). Serve lamb with roasted garlic yogurt.

note **Dukkah is available, ready-made, from delicatessens.**

TANDOORI LAMB WITH FRESH MELON AND COCONUT CHUTNEY

prep & cook time **25 minutes** serves **4** nutritional count per serving **27.3g total fat (13.5g saturated fat); 1601kJ (383 cal); 13.2g carbohydrate; 18.9g protein; 5.7g fibre**

Coarsely grate ½ large firm honeydew melon; drain well. Combine ¼ cup tandoori paste, ¼ cup yogurt and 12 french-trimmed lamb cutlets in large bowl; turn to coat in tandoori mixture. Cook lamb on heated oiled barbecue (or grill or grill plate) until cooked as desired. Meanwhile, combine 1 cup coarsely grated fresh coconut, 2 tablespoons finely chopped fresh mint, 1 tablespoon lemon juice and the grated melon in medium bowl. Serve coconut chutney with lamb and, if desired, pappadums and lemon wedges.

note **If fresh coconut is unavailable, use 1 cup finely shredded dried coconut. The chutney is best if made with a firm (just underripe) honeydew melon.**

grilled chicken, pumpkin and haloumi salad

1 Combine ingredients for rosemary balsamic dressing in screw-top jar; shake well.
2 Combine oil, vinegar, garlic, rosemary and chicken in medium bowl. Cook chicken on heated oiled barbecue (or grill or grill plate) until cooked through; remove from heat, cover.
3 Cook pumpkin and asparagus on barbecue until tender. Transfer to large bowl; cover.
4 Slice cheese thickly; cook on cleaned barbecue until browned both sides.
5 Slice chicken thickly; combine with cheese, rocket and dressing in bowl with pumpkin and asparagus, toss gently.

note Chicken can be marinated overnight, if you like.

BARBECUED PRAWNS WITH CHILLI LIME DRESSING

prep & cook time **35 minutes** serves **4** nutritional count per serving **29.8g total fat (4.2g saturated fat); 1914kJ (458 cal); 3.4g carbohydrate; 44.1g protein; 0.4g fibre**

1.7kg (3½ pounds) uncooked large king prawns (shrimp)
¼ cup coarsely chopped fresh coriander (cilantro)
chilli lime dressing
⅓ cup (80ml) lime juice
⅓ cup (80ml) lemon juice
½ cup (125ml) olive oil
2 cloves garlic, crushed
2 teaspoons caster (superfine) sugar
2 teaspoons sea salt flakes
3 fresh long red chillies, sliced thinly

1 Make chilli lime dressing.
2 Devein prawns, leaving heads and shells intact. Combine prawns in large bowl with half the dressing; cook prawns on heated oiled barbecue (or grill or grill plate).
3 Stir coriander into remaining dressing; serve with prawns.
chilli lime dressing Combine ingredients in small bowl.
Serve with **a sliced pear and leafy green salad.**

GRILLED CHICKEN, PUMPKIN AND HALOUMI SALAD

prep & cook time **50 minutes** serves **4** nutritional count per serving **49.1g total fat (17.2g saturated fat); 3106kJ (743 cal); 12.2g carbohydrate; 62.6g protein; 3.8g fibre**

2 tablespoons olive oil
1 tablespoon balsamic vinegar
2 cloves garlic, crushed
1 tablespoon coarsely chopped fresh rosemary
750g (1½ pounds) chicken thigh fillets
625g (1¼ pound) piece pumpkin, trimmed, sliced thinly
315g (10 ounces) asparagus, trimmed
375g (12 ounces) haloumi cheese
250g (8 ounces) rocket (arugula), trimmed
rosemary balsamic dressing
2 tablespoons olive oil
1 tablespoon balsamic vinegar
1 tablespoon lemon juice
1 tablespoon chopped fresh rosemary

barbecued prawns with chilli lime dressing

CHAR-GRILLED MEDITERRANEAN VEGETABLES

prep & cook time 55 minutes   serves 4   nutritional count per serving 14.8g total fat (2g saturated fat); 1104kJ (264 cal); 22.8g carbohydrate; 6.4g protein; 7.6g fibre

1 medium red capsicum (bell pepper) (200g)
1 medium yellow capsicum (bell pepper) (200g)
1 large red onion (300g), halved, cut into
  wedges
1 small kumara (orange sweet potato) (250g),
  sliced thinly lengthways
2 baby eggplants (120g), sliced thinly
  lengthways
2 medium zucchini (240g), halved lengthways
345g (11 ounces) bottled artichoke hearts,
  drained, halved
100g (3½ ounces) seeded kalamata olives
1 small radicchio (150g), trimmed, leaves
  separated
fresh oregano dressing
¼ cup (60ml) olive oil
2 tablespoons red wine vinegar
2 tablespoons lemon juice
2 cloves garlic, crushed
1 tablespoon finely chopped fresh oregano

1 Make fresh oregano dressing.
2 Quarter capsicums, remove and discard seeds and membranes; cut capsicum into thick strips.
3 Cook capsicum, onion, kumara, eggplant, zucchini and artichoke, in batches, on heated oiled barbecue (or grill or grill plate) until browned and tender.
4 Combine char-grilled vegetables, olives and dressing in large bowl; toss gently. Serve with radicchio.
fresh oregano dressing Combine ingredients in screw-top jar; shake well.

note This robust salad can be made ahead with great success: the flavours of the dressing's fresh oregano and lemon will permeate the grilled vegetables and make them even more delicious. Add radicchio when ready to serve.

char-grilled mediterranean vegetables

note If using bamboo skewers, soak them in cold water for at least
30 minutes before using to prevent them scorching during cooking.

LAMB ON ROSEMARY SKEWERS

prep & cook time **35 minutes (+ refrigeration)** serves **4**
nutritional count per serving **18.6g total fat**
(7.9g saturated fat); 1766kJ (421 cal);
7.7g carbohydrate; 55.5g protein; 0.7g fibre

Cut 1kg (2 pounds) lamb backstrap into 2.5cm
(1 inch) cubes; combine with ¼ cup lemon
juice, 1 crushed garlic clove, 1 tablespoon
olive oil and 2 tablespoons finely chopped
fresh oregano in large bowl. Cover; refrigerate
3 hours or overnight. Remove leaves from
bottom two-thirds of 8 x 15cm (6 inch)
rosemary stalks. Sharpen trimmed ends of
stalks to a point. Thread lamb onto stalks.
Cook skewers on heated oiled barbecue (or
grill or grill plate).
Serve with **tzatziki**.

CHICKEN YAKITORI

prep & cook time **30 minutes** serves **4** nutritional count
per serving **20.4g total fat (6.4g saturated fat); 1643kJ**
(393 cal); 3.8g carbohydrate; 47.1g protein; 0.1g fibre

Combine ¼ cup light soy sauce, 2 tablespoons
mirin, 3 teaspoons white sugar, ½ teaspoon
sesame oil and 1 teaspoon sesame seeds in
small saucepan; stir over medium heat until
sugar dissolves. Thread 12 chicken tenderloins
onto 12 bamboo skewers; brush skewers with
half the sauce mixture. Cook skewers on heated
oiled barbecue (or grill or grill plate). Serve
skewers with remaining sauce mixture.

SKEWERS

FISH GYROS

prep & cook time **30 minutes** serves **4** nutritional count per serving **15.3g total fat (3.2g saturated fat); 1417kJ (339 cal); 21g carbohydrate; 28.1g protein; 2.3g fibre**

Combine 1 tablespoon olive oil with 1 tablespoon red wine vinegar, 2 coarsely chopped medium tomatoes and 45g (1½ ounces) baby rocket leaves (arugula) in medium bowl. Halve 4 long thin white fish fillets (400g); combine fish with 1 tablespoon finely chopped fresh oregano and 1 tablespoon olive oil in medium bowl. Thread fish lengthways onto eight bamboo skewers; cook skewers on heated oiled barbecue (or grill or grill plate). Wrap four 20cm (8 inch) flour tortillas in foil; warm on heated barbecue about 2 minutes, turning once, or until heated through. Serve warm tortillas topped with fish and salad; drizzle with combined ½ cup yogurt and 1 crushed garlic clove.

note **We used flathead fillets in this recipe.**

VEGETARIAN SKEWERS

prep & cook time **20 minutes** serves **4** nutritional count per serving **22.5g total fat (5.1g saturated fat); 1538kJ (368 cal); 19.4g carbohydrate; 20.4g protein; 4.1g fibre**

Combine 2 tablespoons sun-dried tomato pesto, ¼ cup lemon juice and 2 tablespoons olive oil in small bowl. Thread 1 quartered small red onion, 1 coarsely chopped green capsicum (bell pepper), 6 thickly sliced vegetarian sausages and 125g (4 ounces) halved cherry tomatoes alternately, onto eight bamboo skewers. Thread 100g (3½ ounces) coarsely chopped ciabatta bread, 8 cherry bocconcini cheese and another 125g (4 ounces) halved cherry tomatoes, alternately, onto four skewers. Brush skewers with pesto mixture; cook on heated oiled barbecue (or grill or grill plate), brushing with pesto mixture, until skewers are browned lightly. Drizzle skewers with remaining pesto mixture.

CHOCOLATE TART

prep & cook time 1½ hours (+ refrigeration) serves 8
nutritional count per serving 48.1g total fat
(32.7g saturated fat); 2934kJ (702 cal);
59.1g carbohydrate; 7.9g protein; 2.5g fibre

1½ cups (225g) plain (all-purpose) flour
½ cup (110g) caster (superfine) sugar
140g (4¾ ounces) cold butter, chopped
   coarsely
1 egg
1 teaspoon cocoa powder
chocolate filling
2 eggs
2 egg yolks
¼ cup (55g) caster (superfine) sugar
250g (8 ounces) dark (semi-sweet) eating
   chocolate, melted
200g (6½ ounces) butter, melted

1 To make pastry, process flour, sugar and
butter until crumbly; add egg, process until
ingredients come together. Knead dough on
floured surface until smooth. Cover; refrigerate
30 minutes.

2 Roll pastry between sheets of baking paper
(parchment) until large enough to line greased
24cm (9½ inch) round loose-based flan tin. Lift
pastry into tin, press into base and side; trim
edge, prick base all over with a fork. Cover;
refrigerate 30 minutes.

3 Meanwhile, preheat oven to 200°C/400°F.

4 Make chocolate filling.

5 Place flan tin on oven tray; cover pastry with
baking paper, fill with dried beans or rice. Bake
10 minutes. Remove paper and beans carefully
from tin; bake about 5 minutes or until pastry
has browned lightly. Cool.

6 Reduce oven temperature to 180°C/350°F.

7 Pour chocolate filling into pastry case. Bake
about 10 minutes or until filling has set; cool
10 minutes. Refrigerate 1 hour. Serve dusted
with sifted cocoa powder.

chocolate filling Whisk eggs, egg yolks and
sugar in medium heatproof bowl over medium
saucepan of simmering water (don't let water
touch base of bowl) about 15 minutes or until
light and fluffy. Gently whisk chocolate and
butter into egg mixture.

notes Serve tart topped with berries of your choice, if
you like; we used strawberries. Tart can be made a day
ahead; keep refrigerated.

chocolate tart

white chocolate berry trifle

WHITE CHOCOLATE BERRY TRIFLE

prep time **25 minutes (+ refrigeration)** serves **6**
nutritional count per serving **38.4g total fat
(24.3g saturated fat); 2546kJ (609 cal);
49.3g carbohydrate; 10.3g protein; 2.9g fibre**

2 eggs
1⅓ cups (75g) caster (superfine) sugar
250g (8 ounces) mascarpone cheese
⅔ cup (160ml) thickened (heavy) cream
2 tablespoons ground espresso coffee
    granules
1 cup (250ml) boiling water
½ cup (125ml) irish cream liqueur
250g (8 ounces) savoiardi sponge finger
    biscuits
45g (1½ ounces) white eating chocolate,
    grated coarsely
250g (8 ounces) strawberries
155g (5 ounces) raspberries

1 Beat eggs and sugar in medium bowl with
electric mixer until thick and creamy.
2 Beat mascarpone and cream in large bowl
with electric mixer until thick. Fold egg mixture
into mascarpone mixture.
3 Place coffee and the boiling water in coffee
plunger; stand 2 minutes before plunging.
Strain coffee through fine sieve into medium
heatproof bowl; stir in liqueur.
4 Dip half the biscuits, one at a time, briefly in
coffee mixture to soften. Line base of shallow
2-litre (8-cup) serving dish with softened biscuits.
5 Spread half the mascarpone mixture over
biscuits then top with grated chocolate. Slice
half the strawberries thickly; layer over chocolate.
6 Dip remaining biscuits, one at a time, briefly
in remaining coffee mixture to soften. Repeat
layering process with biscuits and mascarpone
mixture. Cover; refrigerate 3 hours or overnight.
7 Slice remaining strawberries thickly; layer
strawberries and raspberries on top of trifle.
Serve topped with more grated white
chocolate, if you like.

note **Trifle is best made a day ahead (up to the end of
step 6); keep, covered, in the refrigerator. Top trifle with
berries and extra chocolate just before serving.**

MARSHMALLOW PAVLOVA

prep & cook time 1¾ hours (+ cooling) serves 8
nutritional count per serving 14g total fat
(9.2g saturated fat); 1095kJ (262 cal);
30g carbohydrate; 3.3g protein; 1.7g fibre

4 egg whites
1 cup (220g) caster (superfine) sugar
½ teaspoon vanilla extract
¾ teaspoon white vinegar
1¼ cups (310ml) thickened (heavy) cream,
  whipped (see notes)
250g (8 ounces) strawberries, halved
¼ cup (60ml) passionfruit pulp

1 Preheat oven to 120°C/250°F. Line oven
tray with aluminium foil; grease foil, dust with
cornflour, shake away excess. Mark 18cm
(7 inch) circle on foil.
2 Beat egg whites in small bowl with electric
mixer until soft peaks form; gradually add
sugar, beating until sugar dissolves between
additions. Add extract and vinegar; beat
until combined.
3 Spread meringue into circle on foil, building
up at the side to 8cm (3 inches) in height.
Smooth side and top of pavlova gently. Using
spatula blade, mark decorative grooves around
side of pavlova; smooth top again.
4 Bake pavlova about 1½ hours. Turn oven
off; cool pavlova in oven with door ajar.
5 Cut around top edge of pavlova (the crisp
meringue top will fall on top of the marshmallow
centre). Serve pavlova topped with whipped
cream, strawberries and passionfruit.

note It is fine just to use 1 x 300ml carton of cream
for this recipe.
Unfilled pavlova can be made up to two days ahead;
store in an airtight container. Top pavlova with cream,
strawberries and passionfruit just before serving.

marshmallow pavlova

ALMOND CRUMBLE NECTARINES

prep & cook time **25 minutes** serves **4** nutritional count per serving **8g total fat (3g saturated fat); 794kJ (190 cal); 23g carbohydrate; 4.1g protein; 5.1g fibre**

Halve and remove stones from 4 nectarines. Combine 2 tablespoons plain (all-purpose) flour, ¼ teaspoon ground cinnamon, 1 tablespoon light brown sugar, 2 tablespoons flaked almonds and ¼ cup muesli in small bowl with 1 tablespoon softened butter. Spoon mixture into hollows in nectarines; place, filling-side up, in baking dish. Pour ½ cup sweet dessert wine into dish, cover; cook on heated barbecue (or grill or grill plate) about 15 minutes or until warmed through.

SWEET LIME MANGOES

prep & cook time **15 minutes** serves **4** nutritional count per serving **1.7g total fat (0.7g saturated fat); 798kJ (191 cal); 35.8g carbohydrate; 4.1g protein; 4.1g fibre**

Slice cheeks from 4 mangoes; score each in shallow criss-cross pattern. Combine 1 tablespoon grated lime rind and 1 tablespoon lime juice; drizzle over each cheek. Sprinkle each with 1 teaspoon light brown sugar. Cook mangoes, cut-sides down, on heated oiled barbecue (or grill or grill plate) until sugar caramelises; serve with ½ cup yogurt.

BARBECUED FRUIT DESSERTS

CHOCOLATY BANANAS

prep & cook time **35 minutes** serves **4** nutritional count per serving **11.6g total fat (10.4g saturated fat); 1639kJ (392 cal); 61.2g carbohydrate; 4.9g protein; 6.1g fibre**

Cut 12cm (4¾ inch) long slit in 4 unpeeled bananas; place bananas on pieces of foil. Chop 155g (5 ounces) dark (semi-sweet) eating chocolate coarsely; divide among slits. Drizzle 2 tablespoons rum into slits; wrap bananas in foil. Cook on heated barbecue (or grill or grill plate) about 30 minutes or until skins blacken. Serve with whipped cream, if desired.

CARAMELISED PEACHES

prep & cook time **15 minutes** serves **4** nutritional count per serving **2.3g total fat (1.4g saturated fat); 481kJ (115 cal); 17.5g carbohydrate; 4.2g protein; 1.8g fibre**

Combine 1 cup yogurt with ¼ teaspoon ground cinnamon and ¼ teaspoon ground cardamom in small bowl. Halve and remove stones from 4 peaches. Cook peach halves, cut-side down, on heated oiled barbecue (or grill or grill plate) until browned. Sprinkle cut-sides with 2 tablespoons light brown sugar; cook, sugared-side down, until sugar bubbles. Serve peaches with spiced yogurt.

PLUMS WITH FRESH HONEYCOMB

prep & cook time **20 minutes** serves **4** nutritional count per serving **0.2g total fat (0g saturated fat); 702kJ (168 cal); 35.9g carbohydrate; 0.9g protein; 3.3g fibre**

Combine ¼ cup caster (superfine) sugar, ¼ cup water and 1 tablespoon madeira in small saucepan; stir over heat until sugar dissolves. Boil gently until syrup is thickened slightly. Halve and remove stones from 8 plums. Brush cut sides with syrup; cook plums, cut-sides down, on heated oiled barbecue flat plate (or grill or grill plate) about 1 minute or until softened. Serve plums with remaining syrup; top with 45g (1½ ounces) coarsely chopped fresh honeycomb.

GRILLED PINEAPPLE WITH COCONUT ICE-CREAM

prep & cook time **15 minutes (+ freezing)** serves **4** nutritional count per serving **26g total fat (19.8g saturated fat); 2128kJ (509 cal); 49.4g carbohydrate; 7.7g protein; 7.3g fibre**

Fold 1 cup toasted shredded coconut and ¼ cup coconut-flavoured liqueur into 1-litre (4-cups) softened vanilla ice-cream; freeze, covered, overnight. Combine 1 tablespoon coconut-flavoured liqueur and 2 tablespoons light brown sugar in large bowl; add 1 thickly sliced large pineapple, toss to coat in sugar mixture. Brown pineapple, both sides, on heated oiled barbecue (or grill or grill plate). Serve with coconut ice-cream.

note **We used Malibu, but any coconut-flavoured liqueur will do.**

BRANDIED PEARS

prep & cook time **15 minutes** serves **4** nutritional count
per serving **0.2g total fat (0g saturated fat); 748kJ
(179 cal); 37.4g carbohydrate; 0.7g protein; 5.3g fibre**

Halve 4 pears lengthways; sprinkle cut sides
with 2 tablespoons brandy then 2 tablespoons
caster (superfine) sugar. Cook pears, cut-sides
down, on heated oiled barbecue (or grill or grill
plate) until golden brown and tender.
Serve with **vanilla ice-cream.**

FRUIT SKEWERS WITH HONEY YOGURT

prep & cook time **40 minutes** serves **4** nutritional count
per serving **8.5g total fat (5.4g saturated fat); 1129kJ
(270 cal); 38.4g carbohydrate; 6.7g protein; 6.1g fibre**

Peel ½ medium pineapple; remove and discard
core. Cut pineapple into 2.5cm (1 inch) lengths;
cut lengths crossways into 2.5cm (1 inch)
pieces. Segment 2 large oranges making sure
to remove all white pith. Hull 250g (8 ounces)
strawberries; cut in half crossways. Peel 2 large
bananas; cut into 2.5cm (1 inch) slices. Thread
fruit, alternating varieties, onto 12 bamboo
skewers; place on oven tray. Combine 30g
(1 ounce) butter, ¼ cup light brown sugar and
1 tablespoon lemon juice in small saucepan;
stir over low heat until butter melts and sugar
dissolves. Pour butter mixture over skewers.
Cook skewers, in batches, on heated oiled
barbecue (or grill or grill plate) until browned
lightly. Serve skewers with 1 cup honey yogurt.

BAKING PAPER also known as parchment paper or baking parchment; a silicone-coated paper primarily used for lining baking pans and oven trays so cakes and biscuits won't stick, making removal easy.

AMERICAN-STYLE PORK RIBS well-trimmed mid-loin ribs. Also known as spareribs.

BASIL an aromatic herb; there are many types, but the most commonly used is sweet, or common, basil.

BEAN SPROUTS also known as bean shoots; tender new growths of assorted beans and seeds germinated for consumption as sprouts.

BEAN THREAD NOODLES: also known as wun sen, made from mung bean paste; also known as cellophane or glass noodles because they are transparent when cooked. White in colour (not off-white like rice vermicelli), very delicate and fine; available dried in various-sized bundles. Soak to soften before use.

BEEF NEW-YORK CUT STEAKS boneless striploin steak.

BREAD
  lavash a flat, unleavened bread of Mediterranean origin.
  mountain soft-textured, thin, dry bread that can be used for sandwiches or rolled up and filled with your favourite filling.
  turkish also known as pide; comes in long (about 45cm) flat loaves as well as individual rounds.

BREADCRUMBS, STALE one- or two-day-old bread made into crumbs by processing.

BUTTER use salted or unsalted (sweet) butter; 125g is equal to one stick (4 ounces).

BUTTER LETTUCE have small, round, loosely formed heads with soft, buttery-textured leaves ranging from pale green on the outer leaves to pale yellow green on the inner leaves.

BUTTERMILK sold alongside fresh milk in supermarkets; despite the implication of its name, it is low in fat.

CAPERS the grey-green buds of a warm climate (usually Mediterranean) shrub; sold dried and salted, or pickled in a vinegar brine. Rinse well before using.

CAPSICUM also known as bell pepper or, simply, pepper. Discard membranes and seeds before using.

CARDAMOM available in pod, seed or ground form. Has a distinctive aromatic, sweetly rich flavour.

CHEESE
  blue mould-treated cheeses mottled with blue veining.
  fetta a sharp, salty tasting, crumbly goat- or sheep-milk cheese with a milky, fresh acidity.
  haloumi a cream-coloured, firm sheep-milk cheese; somewhat like a minty, salty fetta in flavour.
  parmesan a hard, grainy cow-milk cheese.

CHICKEN
  drumette small fleshy part of the wing between shoulder and elbow, trimmed to resemble a drumstick.
  tenderloin thin strip of meat lying just under the breast.

CHILLI available in many types and sizes. Use rubber gloves when seeding and chopping fresh chillies as they can burn your skin. Removing seeds and membranes lessens the heat level.
  green any unripened chilli.
  long red available fresh and dried; any moderately hot, long (about 6cm-8cm) thin chilli.
  red thai small, medium hot and bright red in colour.

CORIANDER also known as pak chee, cilantro or chinese parsley; bright-green leafy herb with a pungent flavour. Stems and roots of coriander are also used in cooking; wash well. Also available ground or as seeds; these should not be substituted for fresh coriander as the tastes are very different.

CORNMEAL often called polenta, to which this ground corn (maize) is similar, albeit coarser. One can be substituted for the other, but textures will vary.

CUMIN a spice also known as zeera or comino.

DUKKAH an Egyptian blend of nuts, spices and seeds; used as a dip when mixed with oil or into mayonnaise, or sprinkled over meats, vegetables or salads as a flavour-enhancer.

EGGPLANT also aubergine.

FISH FILLETS, FIRM WHITE any boneless firm white fish fillet – blue eye, bream, swordfish, ling, whiting or sea perch are all good choices. Check for any small pieces of bone in the fillets and use tweezers to remove them.

GLOSSARY

FIVE-SPICE POWDER a fragrant mixture of ground cinnamon, cloves, star anise, sichuan pepper and fennel seeds. Also known as chinese five-spice.

GINGER also known as green or root ginger; the thick root of a tropical plant.

HONEYCOMB, FRESH is the structure made of beeswax that houses the honey; this edible chewy comb, saturated with honey, is available from speciality food stores, health food stores and delicatessens.

KITCHEN STRING made of a natural product such as cotton or hemp so that it neither affects the flavour of the food it's tied around nor melts when heated.

LAMB BACKSTRAP larger fillet from a row of loin chops.

LAMINGTON PAN 20cm x 30cm (13" x 9" x 2") slab cake pan, 3cm deep.

LEBANESE CUCUMBER slender and thin-skinned. Probably the most popular variety because of its tender, edible skin, tiny, yielding seeds, and sweet, fresh and flavoursome taste.

MINCE known as ground meat.

MIRIN a sweet rice wine used in Japanese cooking; not to be confused with sake.

MUSHROOMS
button small, cultivated white mushrooms with a mild flavour.
enoki clumps of long, spaghetti-like stems with tiny, snowy white caps.
oyster also known as abalone; grey-white mushroom shaped like a fan. Has a smooth texture and a subtle, oyster-like flavour.

shiitake when fresh are also known as chinese black, forest or golden oak mushrooms; are large and meaty and have the earthiness and taste of wild mushrooms. When dried, they are known as donko or dried chinese mushrooms; rehydrate before use.

swiss brown also known as cremini or roman mushrooms, are light brown with a full-bodied flavour. Substitute with button or cup mushrooms.

MUSTARD
dijon a pale brown, distinctively flavoured, mild french mustard.
wholegrain also known as seeded. A French-style coarse-grain mustard made from crushed mustard seeds and dijon-style mustard.

OIL
olive made from ripened olives. Extra virgin and virgin are the best, while extra light or light refers to taste not fat levels.
peanut pressed from ground peanuts; this is the most commonly used oil in Asian cooking because of its high smoke point (capacity to handle high heat without burning).
sesame made from roasted, crushed, white sesame seeds; used as a flavouring rather than a cooking medium.
vegetable sourced from plants rather than animal fats.

ONIONS
green also known as scallion or, incorrectly, shallot; an immature onion picked before the bulb has formed, having a long, bright-green edible stalk.

red also known as spanish, red spanish or bermuda onion; a sweet-flavoured, large, purple-red onion.

shallots also called french shallots, golden shallots or eschalots; small, brown-skinned, elongated members of the onion family. Grows in tight clusters similar to garlic.

PARSLEY, FLAT-LEAF also known as continental or italian parsley.

PRAWNS also known as shrimp.

RADICCHIO a member of the chicory family. Has dark burgundy leaves and a strong bitter flavour. Can be eaten raw or cooked.

RICE VERMICELLI also known as sen mee, mei fun or bee hoon; similar to bean threads, only longer and made with rice flour instead of mung bean starch. Are also known as dried rice noodles. The slightly thicker rice stick noodles may also be used.

ROCKET also known as arugula, rugula and rucola; a peppery-tasting green leaf used similarly to baby spinach leaves. Baby rocket leaves are both smaller and less peppery.

SAMBAL OELEK (also ulek or olek) Indonesian in origin; a salty paste made from ground chillies and vinegar.

SAUCES
barbecue a spicy, tomato-based sauce used to marinate or baste, or as a condiment.
fish also called nuoc nam or nam pla; made from pulverised salted fermented fish, most often anchovies. Has a strong taste and smell, so use sparingly.

hoisin a sweet, thick Chinese barbecue sauce made from salted fermented soya beans, onion and garlic.

soy made from fermented soya beans. Several variations are available in most supermarkets and Asian food stores. We use japanese soy in our recipes.

japanese soy an all-purpose low-sodium soy sauce made with more wheat content than its Chinese counterparts; fermented in barrels and aged. Possibly the best table soy and the one to choose if you only want one variety.

kecap manis a dark, thick sweet soy sauce; the soy's sweetness is derived from the addition of either molasses or palm sugar when brewed.

light soy a fairly thin, pale but salty tasting sauce; used in dishes in which the natural colour of the ingredients is to be maintained. Not to be confused with salt-reduced or low-sodium soy sauces.

oyster Asian in origin, this rich, brown sauce is made from oysters and their brine, cooked with salt and soy sauce, and thickened with starches.

plum a thick, sweet and sour dipping sauce made from plums, vinegar, sugar, chillies and spices.

sweet chilli a comparatively mild, Thai-type sauce made from red chillies, sugar, garlic and vinegar.

teriyaki a Japanese sauce, made from soy sauce, mirin, sugar, ginger and other spices.

vegetarian oyster made from blended mushrooms and soy; available from health food stores and some supermarkets.

SNOW PEAS also called mange tout ('eat all'). Snow pea sprouts are the tender new growths of snow peas.

SOBA a spaghetti-like, pale brown noodle made from various proportions of wheat and buckwheat flours. Both fresh and dried soba can be found in Japanese food shops and some supermarkets.

SPINACH also known as english spinach and, incorrectly, silver beet. Baby spinach leaves are also available.

SUGAR

caster also known as superfine or finely granulated table sugar.

palm also known as nam tan pip, jaggery, jawa or gula melaka; made from the sap of the sugar palm tree. Light brown to black in colour and usually sold in rock-hard cakes. Substitute with brown sugar if unavailable.

white a coarse, granulated table sugar, also known as crystal sugar.

TAMARIND the most popular souring agent in Southern India. The pods are collected, de-seeded and dried. Before cooking, the acid flesh is soaked in water and the juice is squeezed out. Available dried or as a concentrate or paste from Indian food stores and some major supermarkets.

TURMERIC, GROUND the dried root has a peppery, spicy aroma and a bitter, pungent taste. Known for the golden colour it imparts to the dishes of which it's a part.

VIETNAMESE MINT not a mint at all, but a pungent and peppery narrow-leafed member of the buckwheat family; also known as cambodian mint and laksa leaf (daun laksa).

TAHINI a sesame-seed paste.

VINEGAR

brown malt made from fermented malt and beech shavings.

cider (apple cider) made from fermented apples.

WASABI an Asian horseradish sold as a powder or paste.

WATER CHESTNUTS resembles a chestnut in appearance, hence the English name. Small brown tubers with a nutty-tasting, crisp, white flesh. Their crunchy texture is best experienced fresh, however, canned water chestnuts are more easily obtained and can be kept about a month, once opened, under refrigeration.

WATERCRESS a member of the cress family, a large group of peppery greens. Highly perishable, so use as soon as possible after purchase.

WOMBOK also known as peking or chinese cabbage or petsai. Elongated in shape with pale green, crinkly leaves, this is the most common cabbage in South-East Asian cooking.

ZUCCHINI also known as courgette.

CONVERSION CHART

MEASURES

One Australian metric measuring cup holds approximately 250ml, one Australian metric tablespoon holds 20ml, one Australian metric teaspoon holds 5ml.

The difference between one country's measuring cups and another's is within a 2- or 3-teaspoon variance, and will not affect your cooking results. North America, New Zealand and the United Kingdom use a 15ml tablespoon. All cup and spoon measurements are level. The most accurate way of measuring dry ingredients is to weigh them. When measuring liquids, use a clear glass or plastic jug with metric markings.

We use large eggs with an average weight of 60g.

DRY MEASURES

METRIC	IMPERIAL
15g	½oz
30g	1oz
60g	2oz
90g	3oz
125g	4oz (¼lb)
155g	5oz
185g	6oz
220g	7oz
250g	8oz (½lb)
280g	9oz
315g	10oz
345g	11oz
375g	12oz (¾lb)
410g	13oz
440g	14oz
470g	15oz
500g	16oz (1lb)
750g	24oz (1½lb)
1kg	32oz (2lb)

LIQUID MEASURES

METRIC	IMPERIAL
30ml	1 fluid oz
60ml	2 fluid oz
100ml	3 fluid oz
125ml	4 fluid oz
150ml	5 fluid oz
190ml	6 fluid oz
250ml	8 fluid oz
300ml	10 fluid oz
500ml	16 fluid oz
600ml	20 fluid oz
1000ml (1 litre)	1¾ pints

LENGTH MEASURES

METRIC	IMPERIAL
3mm	⅛in
6mm	¼in
1cm	½in
2cm	¾in
2.5cm	1in
5cm	2in
6cm	2½in
8cm	3in
10cm	4in
13cm	5in
15cm	6in
18cm	7in
20cm	8in
23cm	9in
25cm	10in
28cm	11in
30cm	12in (1ft)

OVEN TEMPERATURES

These oven temperatures are only a guide for conventional ovens. For fan-forced ovens, check the manufacturer's manual.

	°C (CELSIUS)	°F (FAHRENHEIT)
Very slow	120	250
Slow	150	275-300
Moderately slow	160	325
Moderate	180	350-375
Moderately hot	200	400
Hot	220	425-450
Very hot	240	475

Measurements for cake pans are approximate only. Using same-shaped cake pans of a similar size should not affect the outcome of your baking. We measure the inside top of the cake pan to determine sizes.

INDEX

If you like this cookbook, you'll love these...

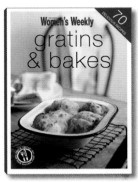

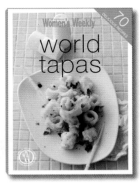

These are just a small selection of titles available in *The Australian Women's Weekly* range
on sale at selected newsagents and supermarkets or online at **www.acpbooks.com.au**